CLASSIC Camaros

BY CLAIRE ROMAINE

INVESTIGATE!

Enslow
PUBLISHING

Please visit our website, www.enslow.com. For a free color catalog of all our high-quality books, call toll free 1-800-398-2504 or fax 1-877-980-4454.

Cataloging-in-Publication Data

Names: Romaine, Claire.
Title: Classic Camaros / Claire Romaine.
Description: New York : Enslow Publishing, 2021. | Series: Classic rides | Includes glossary and index.
Identifiers: ISBN 9781978517875 (pbk.) | ISBN 9781978517899 (library bound) | ISBN 9781978517882(6 pack)
Subjects: LCSH: Camaro automobile–Juvenile literature. | Camaro automobile–History–Juvenile literature.
Classification: LCC TL215.C33 R66 2021 | DDC 629.222'2–dc23

Published in 2021 by
Enslow Publishing
101 West 23rd Street, Suite #240
New York, NY 10011

Copyright © 2021 Enslow Publishing

Designer: Katelyn E. Reynolds
Editor: Therese Shea

Photo credits: Cover, p. 1 (left Camaro) Grzegorz Czapski/Shutterstock.com; cover, p. 1 (middle Camaro) notYourBusiness/Shutterstock.com; cover, pp. 1 (right Camaro), 4 Keith Bell/Shutterstock.com; cover, pp. 1–32 (series chrome font) Mott Jordan/Shutterstock.com; cover, pp. 1–32 (series background) Sylvie Bouchard/Shutterstock.com; p. 5 Imfoto/Shutterstock.com; p. 7 Bob D'Olivo/The Enthusiast Network via Getty Images/Getty Images; p. 8 betto rodrigues/Shutterstock.com; p. 9 (main) BoJack/Shutterstock.com; p. 9 (inset) Phillip W Hubbard/Shutterstock.com; pp. 10, 11 (both), 21 (first generation), 14 National Motor Museum/Heritage Images/Getty Images; pp. 12, 16, 17, 21 (fourth generation) Rich Niewiroski Jr./RichN/Wikipedia.org; pp. 13, 21 (second generation) Ken Morris/Shutterstock.com; pp. 15, 21 (third generation) Sergey Kohl/Shutterstock.com; p. 18 Bryan Mitchell/Getty Images; pp. 19 (main), 21 (fifth generation) Scott Olson/Getty Images; p. 19 (inset) Car Culture ® Collection/Getty Images Plus; p. 21 (sixth generation) PaulLP/Shutterstock.com; p. 23 Jared C. Tilton/Getty Images; p. 24 UPI Photo/General Motors/Alamy Stock Photo; p. 25 Ethan Miller/Getty Images for CaesarsEntertainment; p. 26 Steve Lagreca/Shutterstock.com; p. 27 TIMOTHY A. CLARY/AFP via Getty Images; p. 29 DANIEL KARMANN/DPA/AFP via Getty Images.

Portions of this work were originally authored by Heather Moore Niver and published as *Camaros*. All new material in this edition authored by Claire Romaine.

Printed in the United States of America

Some of the images in this book illustrate individuals who are models. The depictions do not imply actual situations or events.

CPSIA compliance information: Batch #BS20ENS: For further information contact Enslow Publishing, New York, New York at 1-800-398-2504.

Find us on

Contents

WORDS IN THE GLOSSARY APPEAR IN **BOLD** TYPE THE FIRST TIME THEY ARE USED IN THE TEXT.

A CLASSIC Car

When you think of a classic car, what do you picture? Not all old cars are classics. Classic cars have a certain "something" that makes people want to touch their shiny frames and definitely want to get in the driver's seat!

GET THE FACTS!

There have been many different models, or kinds, of Chevrolet Camaros over the years. All used the same platform, called the F-body, until 2009. A platform is the name for a car's overall **design** and its special collection of parts.

The classic car called the Camaro was produced by Chevrolet, a brand in the General Motors (GM) family of cars. In fact, Chevrolet, or Chevy, is still producing Camaros that are certain to be classics. Camaros' cool designs have been turning heads for more than 50 years!

A 1972 CHEVROLET CAMARO IS SHOWN IN WHITE AND BLUE AT A CLASSIC CAR SHOW. THE STRIPES DOWN THE HOOD ARE SOMETIMES CALLED RACING STRIPES.

A CAR FOR *Everyone*

The story of the Camaro begins at another car company. In 1964, the Ford Motor Company issued the wildly successful Mustang. GM realized that it needed to sell a similar car. About two years later, the first Chevy Camaro raced into car showrooms.

GET THE FACTS!

Chevrolet said the name "Camaro" was based on a French word for "friend." Ford workers claimed the meaning was similar to a shrimp-like animal. Chevy workers joked back that it was named after a small, mean animal that ate Ford Mustangs!

SS LOGO

Like the Mustang, the Camaro was a smaller, affordable car. It was considered to be a sports car too. After all, a Camaro was the **pace car** in the 1967 Indianapolis 500! Others thought Camaros were for long, relaxed drives. It was truly a car for everyone.

CARS WITH Muscle

Some Camaro models were called muscle cars. "Muscle car" was the name given to certain midsize vehicles in the 1960s and 1970s that had both power and speed. That usually came from an engine called a big block. In the early days of muscle cars, car owners put in their own engines!

GET THE FACTS!

The 1972 Camaro SS/RS was built the last year Chevy used the special muscle-car engines called big blocks. Muscle cars lost some of their power when they were made to be more **efficient** with fuel and to pollute the air less.

In December 1966, Chevy sped into the muscle-car business. Its Camaro Z/28 had been made to enter the SCCA Trans Am racing series. It was sold to the public because the race's rules required it. The public loved it!

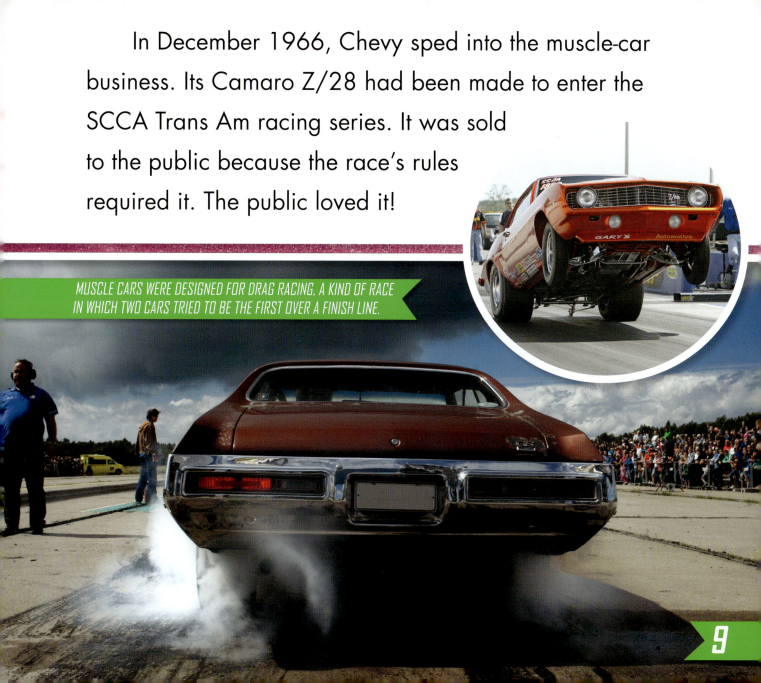

MUSCLE CARS WERE DESIGNED FOR DRAG RACING, A KIND OF RACE IN WHICH TWO CARS TRIED TO BE THE FIRST OVER A FINISH LINE.

FIRST

Generation

Many new cars borrow designs and even parts of other cars. The same was true of the first generation, or class, of Camaros. It was modeled after the Chevy II Nova of 1968. The first Camaros were available as **coupes** or as convertibles, which are cars with a roof that can be lowered or removed.

HOUNDSTOOTH SEATS

GET THE FACTS!

The 1968 Camaro was the first model to have black and white cloth seats with a pattern called houndstooth. The next year, the model known as the Camaro SS/RS convertible had seats covered in orange and black houndstooth. "RS" stands for "Rally Sport."

TAILLIGHTS

FENDER

GRILLE

The 1969 Camaro was sportier than the model from the year before. It had a new **grille**, new **fenders**, and new taillights. This Camaro also had a more angled appearance than earlier Camaros, which were smooth and rounded.

SECOND Generation

LT1 ENGINE OF 1970 CAMARO Z/28

For the second generation of Camaros, beginning with the 1970 model, Chevy went longer and wider. Although this car had a sleeker body and better **suspension**, the design generally stayed the same. Then, in 1978, Chevrolet changed the look. The Camaro got a new front, or nose, with big bumpers under soft plastic.

GET THE FACTS!

The first year that Camaros had T-tops was 1978. A car with a T-top has T-shaped bars on the roof with sections of dark-shaded glass that lift out. Passengers could choose to enjoy the sun and fresh air while driving.

In 1980, Chevy made Camaros that used less gas. However, the less-powerful engines made them unpopular with speed-loving drivers. The 1981 model hardly changed from 1980. It was the last model year for the second generation.

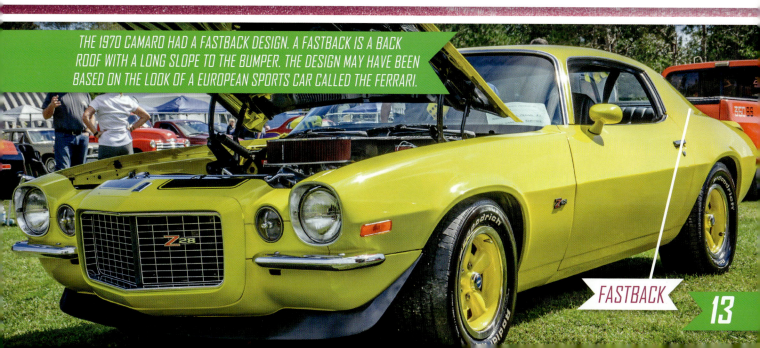

THE 1970 CAMARO HAD A FASTBACK DESIGN. A FASTBACK IS A BACK ROOF WITH A LONG SLOPE TO THE BUMPER. THE DESIGN MAY HAVE BEEN BASED ON THE LOOK OF A EUROPEAN SPORTS CAR CALLED THE FERRARI.

FASTBACK

THIRD Generation

The 1982 Chevy Camaro began a new generation. From engine to frame, it looked like a new car from the past generation and included a **hatchback**. However, reviewers complained the Camaro had lost its power.

1982 CAMARO

GET THE FACTS!

The Camaro IROC-Z borrowed part of its name from the International Race of Champions, or the IROC, which ran almost yearly from 1974 to 2006. Legends such as Mario Andretti, Dale Earnhardt Sr., and Tony Stewart raced in the IROC.

THE IROC-Z WAS AN OPTION, OR CHOICE, PACKAGE FOR THE CAMARO Z28. (THE Z/28 MODEL NAME HAD CHANGED TO Z28—WITHOUT THE SLASH—IN 1972.)

16-INCH WHEELS

Then, in 1985, the Camaro known as the IROC-Z came out. Named after the famous International Race of Champions (IROC), it turned heads with its 16-inch (41 cm) wheels, improved suspension, and a **V-8** engine that provided it with 215 **horsepower**. That same year, *Car and Driver* magazine put the IROC-Z on its Ten Best list.

FOURTH Generation

The model year 1993 began the fourth generation of Camaros with a slick new style—and power too. The Z28 had a mighty LT1 engine with 275 horsepower.

Chevy celebrated Camaro's 30th anniversary with a special 1997 Z28 model. It was white with orange stripes and had orange houndstooth seats, just like the 1969 Indianapolis 500 pace car.

LT1 ENGINE OF 1993 CAMARO Z28

Camaros made between 1999 and 2002 had few major changes, though the engines offered increased horsepower. Sales slowed so much, however, that Chevy canceled production of the Camaro after 2002!

CAR AND DRIVER MAGAZINE CALLED THE 1993 Z28 A "TREMENDOUS PERFORMER."

FIFTH Generation

In 2006, Camaro fans heard the news they had been hoping for. That year, they cheered as Chevy featured a new Camaro model at the North American Auto Show. However, they had to wait a few more years to get behind the wheel.

GET THE FACTS!

A new Camaro model called the ZL1 was offered in 2012. Its V-8 engine boasted an incredible 580 horsepower and pushed the car from 0 to 60 miles (97 km) in 4.1 seconds. It was the fastest and most powerful Camaro model yet.

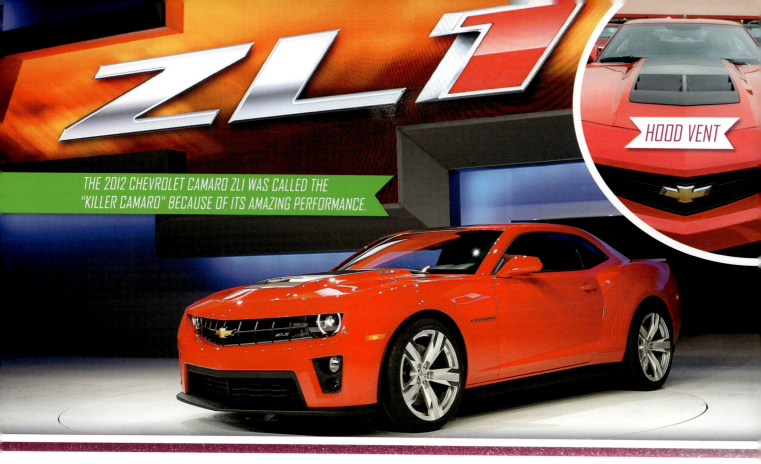

ZL1

THE 2012 CHEVROLET CAMARO ZL1 WAS CALLED THE "KILLER CAMARO" BECAUSE OF ITS AMAZING PERFORMANCE.

The 2010 Camaro SS honored the 1969 model with a similar design, especially the style of the hood and grille. It could really move too. It had a 426-horsepower engine and could go from 0 to 60 miles (97 km) per hour in 4.6 seconds.

SIXTH Generation

The sixth generation of Camaros began with the 2016 model. The Camaro and the Camaro SS options were lighter and smaller than past models. The 2017 ZL1 shared a V-8 engine with the Chevy Corvette Z06, providing a whopping 650 horsepower. The ZL1 could go from 0 to 60 miles (97 km) per hour in 3.4 seconds!

Chevy **engineers** have never stopped perfecting the Camaro, from its style outside to what's under its hood. Recent Camaros sport darker front ends and an option for the 1LE package, promising better braking, steering, handling, and grip.

GET THE FACTS!

Even an older Camaro can be made new. Former NASCAR star Dale Earnhardt Jr. owns an orange 1973 Camaro. He worked on it himself, making it his own. It has a top-of-the-line radio and even a shelf for his dog to sit on!

SIX GENERATIONS OF CAMAROS

FIRST GENERATION (1967–1969)

SECOND GENERATION (1970–1981)

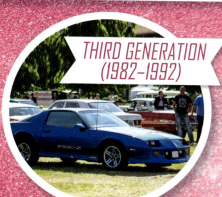
THIRD GENERATION (1982–1992)

FOURTH GENERATION (1993–2002)

FIFTH GENERATION (2010–2015)

SIXTH GENERATION (2016–PRESENT)

ON THE Racetrack

Chevy Camaros have raced successfully since the 1960s. The Camaro ZL1 was introduced to NASCAR in 2018. It was made especially for the high-speed, high-power needs of the race track. With pro driver Austin Dillon at the wheel, it won the Daytona 500 that year!

Not all Camaros on the track are in the actual races. In 1967, the Camaro was asked to be the pace car in the Indianapolis 500 for the first time. Different models of Camaros have been honored as pace cars many more years since.

CAMARO PACE CARS IN THE INDIANAPOLIS 500

1967 — CHEVROLET CAMARO	1969 — CHEVROLET CAMARO
1982 — CHEVROLET CAMARO Z28	1993 — CHEVROLET CAMARO Z28
2009 — 2010 CHEVROLET CAMARO	2010 — 2010 CHEVROLET CAMARO SS
2011 — 2011 CHEVROLET CAMARO CONVERTIBLE	2014 — 2014 CHEVROLET CAMARO Z/28
2016 — 2017 CAMARO SS 50TH ANNIVERSARY EDITION	

AUSTIN DILLON AND HIS CREW CELEBRATE WINNING THE 2018 DAYTONA 500.

CAMARO ZL1

THE COLLECTOR'S Car

JAY LENO

Some car fans collect classic cars, and a few of these fans are famous. TV host Jay Leno has owned several Camaros. He has a special Camaro that Chevy made for him. It was even named after him!

GET THE FACTS!

The Camaro appears in a lot of music! Bands like the Ramones, Weezer, Rascal Flatts, Pearl Jam, and Kings of Leon have songs that feature Camaros. Bruce Springsteen, Keith Urban, Wiz Khalifa, and Gucci Mane have all included the classic car in their songs too.

Chef and TV host Guy Fieri is another loyal Chevy driver. He travels in a bright red 1968 Chevy Camaro SS convertible on his Food Network TV show *Diners, Drive-Ins, and Dives*.

Basketball stars LeBron James and James Harden have also owned custom Camaros, which means the cars were built or changed to suit their tastes.

SOME PEOPLE SAY GUY FIERI'S CAMARO IS THE REAL STAR OF HIS TV SHOW!

CAMAROS AT THE Movies

Camaros have appeared in many movies over the years. Films about racing, like the *Fast and the Furious* movies, were a great stage for the sportiest Camaros.

GET THE FACTS!

Many people wanted to zip down the highway in their own Bumblebee. Chevy announced a 2010 special edition model. This car is fitted with special features, like the symbol of the Autobots, the group of good robots in the movie.

Another series of movies had a Camaro in a starring role. Beginning in 2007, the *Transformers* movies featured a yellow and black Camaro in the role of a robot called Bumblebee. Each film that followed introduced a different Camaro. Bumblebee got his own movie in 2018, in which he appears as a 1977 Camaro. In 2019, a set of four *Transformers* Camaros were sold for a half million dollars!

THE FUTURE OF Camaros

What will the next generation of Chevrolet Camaros look like? How much more powerful will their engines be? What speed records will they break? Will they join the growing number of cars that are becoming electric? Only GM engineers and designers know the answers to these questions.

While we may not know the future, we can enjoy the Camaros that are still on the road and those featured in classic car shows and cruise nights. Their eye-catching designs, revving engines, and colorful histories will attract Camaro fans for years to come!

GET THE FACTS!

Since 1968, Camaro models have been made into the popular Hot Wheels toy cars. To celebrate Hot Wheels' 50th anniversary, Chevy made the exciting announcement in 2017 that it would produce a special Hot Wheels edition Camaro!

PEOPLE WHO GREW UP LOVING HOT WHEELS CARS CAN NOW OWN A REAL-LIFE, ROAD-READY HOT WHEELS CAMARO!

'67 CAMARO

MUSCLE MANIA®

29

Glossary

coupe A two-door car with one section for the seat and another for storage space.

design The plan or form of something.

efficient Having to do with the most effective or purposeful way of doing something.

engineer Someone who plans and builds machines.

fender Any of the corner parts of the body of a car, especially those that surround the wheels.

grille A metal screen on the front of a car that allows cool air into the engine.

hatchback A car design in which the trunk lid is replaced with a door that opens upward and usually includes the rear window.

horsepower A unit used to measure the power of an engine.

pace car A car that leads racers around the track to warm up their engines but does not join in the race.

suspension A system of springs and other parts on a car that reduces the shaking and bumping caused by uneven surfaces.

V-8 A kind of engine that has two sets of four chambers at an angle to each other.

FOR MORE INFORMATION

BOOKS

Mason, Paul. *American Supercars: Dodge, Chevrolet, Ford*. New York, NY: PowerKids Press, 2019.

Oachs, Emily Rose. *Chevrolet Camaro Z28*. Minneapolis, MN: Bellwether Media, 2017.

Worms, Penny. *Sports Cars*. Mankato, MN: Smart Apple Media, 2016.

WEBSITES

Camaro
www.chevrolet.com/camaro
Keep up with the latest Camaro models and news.

Hot Rods and Muscle Cars
www.history.com/specials/hot-rods-and-muscle-cars
Read about these cool cars on the History website.

Index